Squirrel Wood

By
Ken Mackenzie

Prepared for Print in 2017 by HawkMedia

53 Stucley Road
Bideford
Devon
Ex393eq

© Ken Mackenzie 2017

Illustrations by Sue Hawkins

ISBN-13: 978-1978345959

ISBN-10: 197834595X

Squirrel Wood

All rights reserved. No part of this publication may be reproduced, stored in a retrieval system, or transmitted in any form by any means electronic, mechanical, photocopying, scanning, recording or otherwise, without the prior written permission of the author.

Website: www.hawkmedia.co.uk

Email:admin@hawkmedia.co.uk

Telephone: 01237 476238

About The Author

" KENNY MAC,"
Torquay children's author.

One bright sunny day in squirrel wood, all the grey squirrels were going about their daily jobs. All the daddy grey squirrels were out finding nuts and berries....

....*all the mummy grey squirrels were tidying up....*

....and all the little baby squirrels were in the trees running around and having fun....

All the squirrels knew each other and they all had their own special tree branches where they lived. Nothing very exciting ever happened in Squirrel Wood but it was a very happy and peaceful place.

It was now lunchtime and all the baby squirrels were home....

….They had finished eating their nuts and berries and were settling down for their afternoon naps….

....Everything in Squirrel Wood was very quiet when all of a sudden, there was a rustling in the trees. A mummy, a daddy and two baby squirrels appeared in the clearing....

....One of the grey squirrels in the tree tops heard the noise and came out to see what it was....

He couldn't believe his eyes; strange squirrels had wandered into their woods, and they were RED. He had never seen a red squirrel before. How strange they looked!

He ran down his tree and stood in front of them, "Who are you and what do you want in our wood?"

The red daddy squirrel said, "We have nowhere to live and no food for our children. Could we stay here?"

"NO," said the grey squirrel in a very loud voice. "You can't stay here! These are our woods and anyway, you're not grey, you are a funny red colour."
All the other squirrels heard the noise and came out to see what was going on. They were very surprised to see the red strangers.

Some of the daddy squirrels stood in a line and said, "You're not welcome here!"

"But why not?" asked the red daddy squirrel. "Is it because we are strangers?"

"No," said one, "it's because you're different. You're a funny red colour. We don't want funny red squirrels in our wood. We are all grey."

It was then that some of the mummy squirrels stepped forward, "What delightful children," they said. "Of course you're welcome here!"

13

The daddy squirrels were very angry for they didn't want strangers in their woods, especially red ones. All the squirrels began arguing and Squirrel Wood wasn't very quiet or peaceful anymore.

It was getting very noisy with everyone arguing. Some didn't mind if the red strangers stayed and others didn't want them to stay.

The arguing went on for a long, long time when one baby grey squirrel stepped forward.

He took the two baby squirrels by the hand and said, "You can come with me and I will give you some food and we can play in the trees after if you like."

The daddy squirrels stood and stared as the little grey squirrel took the red squirrel babies off to his tree. They felt very, very ashamed for it had taken a little baby to show them that even if you're a stranger and even if you're a different colour, you're still a squirrel.

All the squirrels then decided that it was alright for the red squirrel family to stay…

...and they even gave them a tree to call their own....

Now, grey squirrels and red squirrels all live happily together.

The End

Printed in Great Britain
by Amazon